Unintentional Humor

Humor

Celebrating the Literal Mind of Autism

Written By: Brent Anderson &
              Linda Gund Anderson

Cartoons By: Alan J. Lewis &
                 Brett Bednorz

Please contact us at:
www.CelebrateAutism.com
Email: CelebrateAutism@gmail.com

ISBN: 978-0-9834509-6-2

Printed in the U.S.A.
GP Gund Publishing
P.O. Box 24259
Ventura, CA 93002
805-223-5130

ABOUT AUTISM

Autism is the fastest growing serious developmental disability in the U.S.A. The CDC quotes diagnosis rates as 1 in 110 children and 1 in 70 boys with its prevalence continuing to rise at astounding rates. A new study, published in the May, 2011 American Journal of Psychiatry, finds rates as high as 1 in 38 children.

Autism is defined as a range of neurological and psychological conditions known as Autism Spectrum Disorders (ASD). The spectrum ranges from mild to severe, providing a wide variety of symptoms and challenges. Collectively, ASD has common characteristics which often include; impaired social interaction, difficulty reading social cues and a literal interpretation of language.

As we **Celebrate Autism** we hope to increase awareness, acceptance & understanding and ultimately improve the lives of those with ASD and the people who love and care for them.

3

<u>OUR STORY</u>

My mother's intuition told me there was something different about my 2 1/2 year old son. People thought I was overreacting, friends said he didn't play well with others, pediatricians told me he would outgrow it, preschools wouldn't accept him and some questioned my parenting. I read dozens of child rearing books, but still had no insight into what I was dealing with. I spent every day searching for answers, feeling overwhelmed, scared, and worried about my sweet little boy, Brent. Discouraged by the medical system & frustrated that other parents weren't having these issues, I was determined to get an explanation. The question remained, what was the matter with my son?

Luckily, a move to Boulder, CO in 1989 provided me access to the staff at the Developmental Disabilities Center. In one appointment, I learned that I was actually not a "bad mother", but instead, my child's biggest advocate. My son did have developmental disabilities, and was in need of intensive therapy and support. Although, not diagnosed with Asperger's for another 10 years, I was relieved that Brent would receive the treatment he needed, and extremely grateful for the support that I would also receive.

In 1990, Brent began working with speech therapist, Andrea Mann. Her expertise taught me about Brent's struggles with communication and language. We discussed the need for a book to teach the meaning of common words and phrases. Although it has taken over 20 years to complete, **Unintentional Humor; Celebrating the Literal Mind of Autism,** is the result.

Writing this book has transformed my relationship with Brent. We now have an open dialogue about how his mind interprets language. We discuss our differences & laugh at the disparities in our worlds. I have come to believe that I am the one with the skewed interpretation of language, not Brent. He sees the words as they are written, in their pure form. In either case, the misinterpretations often cause frustration and pain. We hope that **Unintentional Humor** will improve communication for everyone touched by the world of Autism.

ABOUT THE AUTHORS

Brent Anderson is the inspiration for this book. He worked closely with our artists to ensure that our graphics represent how he "saw" the words. Brent is developing ideas for animated T.V. shows and comic books. He volunteers at the Humane Society in Ojai, CA and maintains his lifelong love of animals. He lives in Ventura, CA.

Linda Gund Anderson is an advocate for children with disabilities. She fought for classroom accommodations, inclusion & more therapy in public schools. Linda has been an effective fundraiser and is committed to raising funds for local Autism groups and helping to increase the National research budget for Autism.

ACKNOWLEDGMENTS

There are so many people to thank for their "unknowing" contribution to our book. Brent's incredible teachers and therapists: Francess Reda, Chris Fukai, Lizzie Feeney, Mark Twaragowski, Amy Thompson, Mark Wood, Philippe Ernewein & the entire staff of Denver Academy Dr. Patrick Bacon, Tracey Anderson, Diane Heidel and Norma Joosten. The supportive staff of TIL in Ventura, CA & Larry Rice, Tri-Counties Regional Centers.

Special thanks to our cartoonists and designers:
Alan J. Lewis and Brett Bednorz
and
Special Contributor: Andrea Mann, M.A. CCC

Jenny Anderson, the best sister and daughter anyone could ever have. She is an invaluable resource, source of support and an important contributor to our book.

All of our family and friends, who support and accept Brent and embrace his world of **Unintentional Humor**.

BRENT'S STORIES

YOU'RE DRIVING ME UP THE WALL

STOP BUGGING ME

When I heard kids in my class say,
"Stop Bugging Me"...
I began looking
around for the bugs.

LEANING TOWER OF PIZZA

I was excited when our family went on a trip to Europe and I got to see to the,

"Leaning Tower of Pizza"

I was really confused when we got there and they didn't sell pizza.

Mom explained to me that it is called the, Leaning Tower of Pisa.

OOPS!!!

COUCH POTATO

I spent the weekend with my friend Jordan.

I didn't understand why he called his brother Patrick a "**Couch Potato.**"

BASEBALL BAT

I was worried that they played
with real bats.....

SCHOOL OF FISH

PLAYING MUSIC BY EAR

CAN OF WORMS

I heard my Mom talking with Holly about having the
neighborhood homeowners meeting at our house.
She reminded her of the issues at last year's meeting
and Mom said, **"Let's not open that can of worms."**

I shouted from the other room,
"Yeah, that would be gross."

DOG EARED PAGES

I heard my Grandpa say that he gets upset when people **DOG EAR** pages of his books.....I looked at some of his books and never saw any dog ears in there.

MONKEY BUSINESS

I always wondered what kind of
businesses monkey's had.

IN A NUTSHELL

I don't understand why people use
this saying so often.

How does someone get in a nutshell?

<u>LET THE CAT OUT OF THE BAG</u>

My Mom was planning
a surprise party for one of Jenny's friends.
She spent a lot of time on the phone
making plans for the big day.

She told us we weren't allowed
to tell anyone about the upcoming surprise.

I heard her say to Jenny,
"We have to make sure not to
Let The Cat Out of The Bag."

I was really confused by that and asked,

"Mom why would someone put their
cat in a bag?"

SEA HORSE

When we went on our first trip to the beach,
I really hoped we would find a
"Sea Horse".

I was very disappointed when we did not.

THE MONKEY BARS

I was afraid of the **"Monkey Bars"**
when I was in Elementary School.
I never went on them because I wasn't
sure if I was going to turn into a monkey.

25

SURFING THE WEB

IT'S RAINING CATS & DOGS

GOLF NUT

People say that
my Uncle Jim is a
"GOLF NUT"

<u>JELLYFISH</u>

I knew that Jellyfish lived in the ocean,

but I still thought that they made Jelly.

BANK HOLD UP

I heard about this on the news, but I didn't understand how anyone was strong enough to do that.

<u>FUNNY BONE</u>

I came into the kitchen
laughing and told Jenny,
"I think I found my
"Funny Bone".

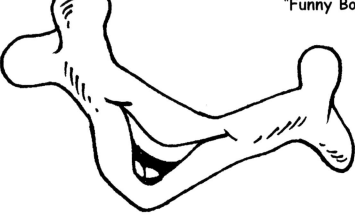

She asked me if I could help her find hers.

CARD SHARK

I learned on a family trip, that Jason
is considered a real
"Card Shark"!!

BROKEN RECORDS

My Mom usually has the news on when
I am eating breakfast in the morning.

One day I asked her why the weather man was
talking about people "**Breaking Records**".

TURN INTO A PRUNE

I always liked to spend a lot of time playing with my toys in the bathtub.

One night I told Mom I would not take baths anymore. When she asked me why I said,

"Because Grandma told me
that if I spend too much time in the bath,
I will turn into a Prune, and I don't want
that to happen."

CONFUSING STREET SIGNS

On a drive through Utah, I was excited when I saw this sign because I really wanted to see the Eagles.

Mom said, she hoped we didn't.

When I saw this sign on a trip to the mountains I said, "Why would someone want to stand on this road?"

Other confusing signs:

FAVORITE TEAMS

My family watched a lot of sporting events together.
I only liked the teams
that had names of animals.

THE BEARS

THE BULLS

<u>Some of my other favorite teams:</u>

Colorado Buffaloes	Anaheim Mighty Ducks
Miami Dolphins	Washington Huskies
San Jose Sharks	Arizona Diamondbacks

CHILL OUT

I don't understand why people say this
when it's not even warm outside.

HALF OFF

When I was young, I was confused
by the signs
in toy stores that said:

50% OFF

I asked Mom,
"Why would someone want only
HALF of that toy?"

I was sure it wouldn't work any more
if it was broken in half.

MOM STORIES

(written by Linda)

<u>YOU'RE IN THE DOG HOUSE</u>

One day I found Brent
wandering around the back yard.
He was looking in the bushes and
around the area where our
dog usually sleeps.

I came outside and asked
him what he was doing.

He replied, "Looking for Dad."

I reminded him that
Dad was at work.

Confused, he replied,
"You said he was in the
DOG HOUSE."

COMPUTER MOUSE

Brent came home after spending the day at Countryside Montessori School with Jenny.

I asked him what fun jobs he had done that day. He said he was really happy that they had worked on the computers.

He added, " Except I could never find out where the **Computer Mouse** was."

ONLY A $5.00 BILL

I took Brent to the store to buy a snack. I wanted him to try and pay for it on his own. He picked out a soft drink and a bag of chips. The clerk told him that his total was $2.65.

He looked at me and said, "Mom, I don't have that much. **I only have a $5.00 bill.**"

<u>GIVE ME A RING</u>

The kids and I were at the mall when I ran into my friend, Mary. We talked for awhile, and before we left, I told her that she should **give me a ring** in the next few days.

When we got in the car, Brent asked,

"Why is Mary going to give you a **RING?**"

UNIVERSITY OF PUGET SOUND

48

<u>BRINGING HOME THE RAIN</u>

Jenny had recently arrived home after her
first semester of college in
Tacoma, Washington.

The three of us had gone into a book store
under sunny skies. When we were leaving
the store we were surprised by
an unexpected rainstorm.

Running to the car, Jenny said,
"I can't believe I brought the rain
with me from Washington."

After being in the car for a few minutes,
Brent looked at her and asked,

**"Jenny, did you really bring the rain
home with you?"**

FROG IN YOUR THROAT

Brent came home from school and shared, "Mr. Best told us that he was having a hard time talking in class, because he had a **frog in his throat.**"

"I looked at him all day, but I never saw the frog."

50

SPEAK UP IF YOU WANT TREATS

Brent was given clear instructions for watching our dog,
Jessie over the weekend. I left him notes telling
him when to feed her, walk her, etc.
I even bought a special box of dog biscuits
for him to give her while I was gone.

When I returned home,
I was upset to find
the box of dog biscuits
had not been opened.
I asked Brent why
he hadn't given
Jessie any
treats.

His response, "She didn't say she wanted any."

51

STARVING STUDENTS

A few years ago on Mother's Day,
my 19 year old daughter, Jenny,
and my 21 year old son, Brent,
and I went out to a nice dinner and a play.

As I pulled out my credit card to pay
the dinner bill, Jenny said,
"I'm sorry Mom, we should be buying
your dinner since today is Mother's Day.
But, since we are both
Starving College Students,
we can't afford to."

Brent quickly chimed in,
"Jenny I am not starving myself,
I've actually been gaining weight."

<u>CLOUD NINE</u>

After learning about my promotion at work,
I told Brent that I felt like I was on "**Cloud Nine**".

He went outside, looked up at the sky and asked,
"Which cloud is that, Mom?"

DON'T LET THE BED BUGS BITE

My kids stayed at home with a babysitter so that I could go to the movies with my friend, Kate. When I got home Brent was not in his bed, and I found him asleep on the floor in my room.

I woke him up and asked why he was sleeping on the floor.

He replied, "I am afraid of the bugs."

"There aren't any bugs in your bed, sweetie. What makes you think that?"

Because the babysitter told me;

"GOODNIGHT, SLEEP TIGHT, DON'T LET THE BED BUGS BITE."

<u>I AM NOT A CHICKEN</u>

Brent came home from school in tears. I sat him down and asked what had made him so upset.

Through his sobs, he explained that at recess he was afraid to go on the big slide. Some of the kids then started calling him a chicken.

"Mom, I told them **I am not a chicken-** I am a BOY!"

PULLING MY LEG

One day Brent asked me,
"Why does Uncle Mac keep telling me he's
Pulling My Leg?"

FIRED FROM YOUR JOB

I picked Brent up from a friend's
house and he was very upset.
He had overheard a phone conversation
that Matt's mom was having with
one of her friends.

He said she was crying, as she
explained that her husband had
been fired from his job.

Brent was really confused and
asked me if Matt's dad was going to
get hurt when he was,

"Fired!"

EAT LIKE A HORSE

After hearing my Uncle use this expression,
Brent explained in great detail
how the horses at the
Colorado Therapeutic Riding Center were fed.

FISHING TACKLE

Brent had learned about tackling from watching football, however, trying to explain this was challenging.

<u>WHAT TIME?...WHAT DAY?...</u>

I called Brent to find out what date his summer school class was ending so I could plan our summer vacation.

My first question was,
   "When does your class end?"

His response,
      "It ends at 3 O'Clock."

I took a deep breath and asked my second question.
"Please tell me what **DAY** your class ends."

His reply,
"It ends on Thursday."

OH, YOU WANT THE DATE...

Frustrated, I asked him, (in the proper way),
"Brent, what is the **DATE**
that your class ends?"

Quickly he responded,
"July 23rd."

PARKING RATES

Brent and I were picking up my friend Robin at the airport. We parked in the short term parking lot and went inside to meet her.
As we were leaving, he noticed that the sign at the payment booth said:

PARKING RATES:

$1.00 per ½ hour

$8.00   Maximum

After looking at the sign for quite awhile he asked,

"Where do you park if you need to stay at the airport for more than 4 hours?"

CATCHING RAYS

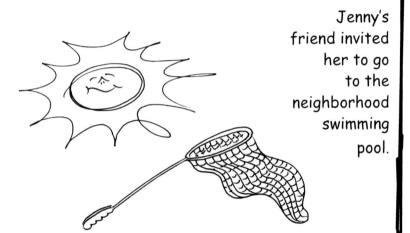

Jenny's friend invited her to go to the neighborhood swimming pool.

Brent called me at work to ask if I knew where our butterfly net was.
"Why?" I asked him.

Jenny said that she and Melanie are going to
"Catch Rays."

BACKSEAT DRIVER

When Jenny was taking her Master Drive classes she became quite opinionated about my driving techniques. One day I told her she was a, **"Backseat Driver."**

Brent asked me, "How can she do that Mom? She can't even reach the pedals."

THE TEACHER SAID SO

Brent was not always a popular kid in the classroom.
He became known as the, 'Little Dictator'
because of how literally he interpreted the
teacher's instructions to the class.

When the teacher would say, "Let's turn off our
computers and come back to our desks,"
Brent often took it upon himself to turn off
all the computers...
even when classmates were still using them.

When the art teacher would tell students to
put away their projects,
Brent would often take brushes
and paints out of other student's hands....

He often got in trouble because of this behavior,
but his reply was always the same,
"The teacher said so..."

POT LUCK DINNER

I told Brent that we had been invited to a Pot Luck dinner, and I was having a hard time trying to decide what I was going to bring.

Later that evening he said,

"I don't know what you're worried about Mom,"

"Aren't you supposed to bring your
LUCKY POT
to the Pot Luck dinner?"

WRONG SIDE OF THE BED

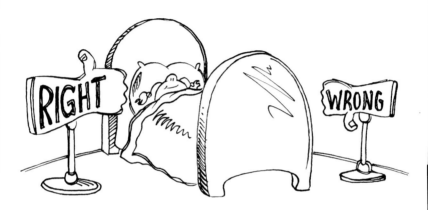

One morning during breakfast
Jenny was in a particularly bad mood.
I asked her if she had gotten up on the
"WRONG SIDE OF THE BED".

Brent quickly ran upstairs to his room
and shouted down,
"Mom, how do I know if I got up on the
Right or the Wrong side of the bed?"

CAT GOT YOUR TONGUE?

When Brent spends the entire
day with his Grandfather, it often includes
going out to eat with some of his friends.

During one of their outings, they
encountered my father's retired business associate.
Trying to engage him in conversation,
Mr. Simpson asked Brent what school he attended.

Brent hesitated a bit before he
came up with the answer.

My Dad then said,
"What's the matter, boy...
"Cat Got Your Tongue"?

Brent said, "What Cat?"

THE FUNNY FARM

Brent was watching a T.V. show and a character commented that their neighbors needed to go to the **"Funny Farm"**.

He asked me if I thought our neighbors should go to the Funny Farm.

My answer required a lot of explaining.

ELBOW GREASE

A good friend came over to help with some home
improvement projects at my house and
I asked if Brent could be his helper.

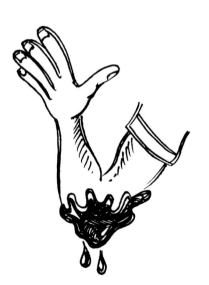

Encouraging him to work
a little bit harder,
he suggested that
Brent needed to use more
Elbow Grease.

Brent said,
"Uncle Mike, where do
I get some of that
Elbow Grease
that you are using?"

<u>UNDER THE WEATHER</u>

I had plans to meet my friend Tracy for dinner.
Around 4:00, I received a call
from her husband telling me that she wasn't
feeling well and needed to cancel.

Brent overheard me say,
"Nathan, please tell Tracy I am sorry that she is
"Under the Weather".

When I got off the phone I saw
Brent looking curiously out the window.

He asked me, "Why did you say that
Tracy is Under the Weather?"

"It looks sunny outside..."

I GOT STOOD UP

Brent saw Jenny on her bed crying
and asked her what was the matter.

"Henry **Stood Me Up,**" she said.
Brent replied,
"Then why are you lying down?"

<u>GIVING AWAY THE BRIDE</u>

Our family was watching a T.V. program
that featured a large celebrity wedding
that was being held in our hometown.

The announcer was providing descriptions of
the church, the flowers, the bride's dress,
and the families of the bride and groom.
She gave details of the wedding party while showing
video of the bride walking down the aisle.

Then the announcer commented,
"and the **Bride was given away by her Father**."

Brent, who was watching the show
with me said,

"THAT'S MEAN"....

LET'S HAVE T.V. DINNERS

My Mom picked up Brent and Jenny
to take them out to dinner and
then have them sleep over at her house.
When they got to the restaurant,
they found out the kitchen was experiencing
problems and was not able
to serve any customers.

Knowing the kids were hungry and she didn't
have anything prepared at her house,
she suggested that they go to the grocery
store and pick up T.V. dinners.

Brent said,
"Namie, I've never eaten a
T.V. for dinner before."

BROKEN HEART

My sister and I went to lunch at the mall. She was very upset about the recent breakup with her boyfriend. She told story after story of their difficulties and how many times he had broken her heart.

Later at home Brent asked me,
"When is Aunt Beth going to the hospital
to **fix her broken heart?**"

YOU LOST A TOOTH

One evening at dinner, Jenny announced that earlier in the day she had, **"Lost a Tooth."**

Brent quickly jumped up from the table and ran into the play room. I watched him start pulling toys out of the toy box.

Frustrated, I said, "Brent, what are you doing?"

His response, "Looking for Jenny's lost tooth."

CAR POOLS

DUCK TAPE

NO CRYING OVER SPILLED MILK

Jenny came home from school very upset.
She told me that there had been a
fight at lunchtime
between some of her friends.

I told her that while things seemed
difficult right now, she should try
not to worry about what happened at school.
I explained that in a day or two they would
forgive each other and it wouldn't
seem important anymore.

I must have used the expression,
"There's No Use Crying Over Spilled Milk,"
because Brent ran into the kitchen asking;

"Who Spilled the Milk?"

CLOSE THE WINDOW

I got home from work and found the windows open during a pouring rainstorm.

When I walked in the family room Brent was watching T.V., unaware of the rain coming in the house.

Angrily I said, "I thought I told you to close the windows if it started raining."

He said, "You did, Mom, but **you didn't tell me which ones!!"**

CUT A RUG

One day Brent asked me what the expression, **"Cut A Rug"** means.

He laughed after I explained it to him.

A few weeks later, when I was getting ready
to go to a party he said,
"Don't forget to take your scissors, Mom."
I asked him, "Why?"

He snickered and said,
"So you can **Cut a Rug**!!"

3 STRIKES AND YOU'RE OUT

With close friends involved in
Major League Baseball, Brent has been
fortunate to attend many
Colorado Rockies baseball games.

Over the years, I had explained the rules
to him, and I assumed that he had a
good understanding of the game.

When we started working on this book,
he shared how he always felt sorry
for the baseball players that were
"Thrown Out."

He really thought the players
left the game and went home.

TIME FLIES WHEN HAVING FUN

My kids spent the day with my good friend, Meg. After a few hours she looked at her watch and commented, "I can't believe that it's almost time take you home. I guess it's true that,

"Time Flies When You're Having Fun".

Brent heard her say this, looked around, and said, "Where? I don't see it."

<u>WILD GOOSE CHASE</u>

I took the kids to the mall to find some items my
friend Liz wanted for her birthday.

We went from store to store, asking if anyone
knew what stores might sell the items we needed.
We received a lot of different answers,
but never found what we were looking for.

After four hours, I told the kids
that I felt like we had been sent on
a **"Wild Goose Chase"**
through the mall.

Brent had a puzzled look on his face, and said,
"I didn't see any geese at the mall today.
Did you Jenny?"

PIG OUT

HAPPY CAMPER

STORIES SHARED BY OTHERS

PIECE OF CAKE

After one student called their spelling test a
"PIECE OF CAKE,"

other classmates began complaining,
"I didn't get a piece of cake."

STOP THE HORSEPLAY

A boy asked his mother, "What does Daddy mean when he tells us to, **Stop that Horseplay?**"

DRESS THE TURKEY

While discussing
with my Grandmother
what recipes we
should make for
Thanksgiving
dinner,
she asked
me what I liked
to use to dress
the Turkey.

My son Andrew said,

"Grammy, why would
you want to
Dress The Turkey?"

99

<u>ALL EARS</u>

I happened to be working in my daughter's
3rd grade classroom on a day they were
having a guest speaker.

I heard the teacher tell the kids that
they needed to be
"ALL EARS"
during the presentation.

I wasn't surprised when I saw my
daughter raise her hand and
ask Mrs. Arnold,
"Where do I get some more ears?"

I felt sad when the other kids
laughed at her.

<u>RECYCLED CHRISTMAS TREES</u>

A few days
after Christmas,
my husband and I were
discussing which one
of us was going
to take our Christmas
tree to the
Recycling Center.

Our son, Cody, thought for
awhile and then said,

"I wonder if we will
get the same tree
again next year..."

FINGER FOODS

A mom came home from work exhausted and told her kids she was too tired to make dinner.

"Let's just have **finger foods** tonight," she suggested.
Horrified, her daughter shouted,
"Mom, why would you make us do that?"

POOR TEACHER

On the last day of school, my son, Sam
was saying good-bye to his 4th grade teacher.

I listened while he told her about our
summer plans. At the end of the conversation,
I was surprised to hear him say that
when he grows up he is
planning on giving her money.

When we got to the car I asked him,
"Why did you tell Mrs. Johnson that
you are going to give her money ?"

"Because I heard you tell
Grandma that she is a,
"Poor Teacher."

HIT THE SACK

My kids were having a sleep over at our neighbors.

After watching TV and playing games until 10:00, Sharon came in to tell them it was time to **"Hit the Sack."**

My son asked his sister, "What does she mean by that?"

THE LOCKER ROOM

My daughter loved learning to swim.
It had become a favorite activity of hers
before I took her to the local recreation center
to use their new indoor pool.

The new pool rules required everyone to
shower before getting in the water.
I told my daughter that we had to go
into the Locker Room and rinse
off before we could go swimming.

She started crying and said,

"Mom, I don't want to go in the
LOCK HER ROOM."

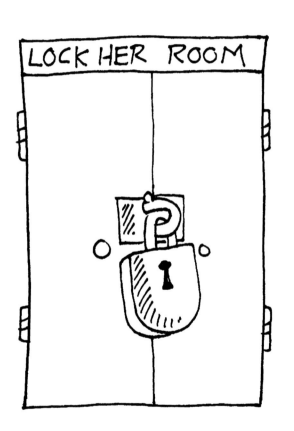

FARMER IN THE DELL

AIRPLANE HANGARS

CAT FISH

While at a Seafood Restaurant, my daughter saw
that they had
Catfish on the Menu...

I heard her giggle and whisper, "MEOW."

<u>GROSS NATIONAL PRODUCT</u>

A father shared his story of
dinner table conversation
he recently had with his daughter.

My daughter and I discussed how
confused she was
by a topic they had discussed
in her High School Economics class-

the "**Gross National Product**."

My daughter asked me,
"Is that because all of
the products are gross?"

CHICKEN WITH IT'S HEAD CUT OFF

My son went to stay with our friends
the Ryan's in San Diego for the weekend.
It was a big deal because he was going
to visit all by himself.

He called home one night because he was
confused about something Lynn
had said at dinner that evening.

"She said when she was at work she
was running around like a
Chicken with It's Head Cut off.."

"Why would she say that, Mom?"

LAME DUCK

A teacher shared the story of a student who came into her office very confused by what he had heard in History class.

"We learned that after a certain amount of time, our President becomes a **"Lame Duck"**.

Confused, he asked me, "Why would the President turn himself into a duck?"

WE'LL BE THERE WITH BELLS ON

My sister called to tell me she was finally
marrying her long time boyfriend.
"We'll be there with bells on..." I told her.

Later that week, my daughter and I went shopping
for outfits to wear to the wedding.

She asked, "Mom, when do we get the bells
we're going to wear?"

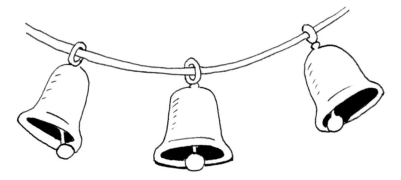

PLAYING BADMINTON

When my son learned about the game Badminton,
he was very upset when he heard that you are
supposed to hit the **"Birdy"**!!

OUR FOUR FATHERS

My nephew was staying at our house and I was helping him with his homework.
We were discussing the constitution and how it had been written by the Forefathers of our Country.

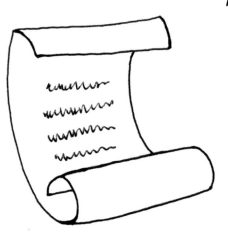

My son must have been listening to our conversation, because he said to me at bedtime,

"I can remember Jefferson, Lincoln and Adams, but who was the fourth one of the **FOUR FATHERS?**"

ROAD CLOSED

We loaded the entire family into the car for a weekend trip to the mountains.

About an hour outside of town, my husband said, "The weather is so bad, I'm afraid they may close the road."

My son asked, "Mom, how do they set up the doors?"

BULL IN A CHINA CLOSET

I HATE CHANGE

My daughter overheard my friend Colleen telling me,
"I don't like change."

Thinking she knew a good solution, she said to her,
"Why don't you use your credit card?"

GRANDPARENT STORIES

Stories shared after spending time
with their Grandparents.

"Grandma always knows
what we are doing
because she has eyes in
the back of her head."

"Grandma and
Grandpa lived when
they didn't even have
television.
What do you think
they did all the
time?"

"Did you know that
Grandma had to walk
"Uphill Both Ways"
to go to school?

"Grandpa said
that things
today don't
amount to a
"Hill of Beans"?

THAT GIRL IS HOT

My brother called to tell me about the humorous situation that occurred while he was at a restaurant with my son. My brother commented that the waitress was, "**Hot**".

My son replied, "It is hot in here, why doesn't she do something to cool down?"

<u>DOWN IN THE DUMPS</u>

We were doing projects around the house, and my
husband asked my son to ride in the car
with him to the local dump.

My son asked,
"Is that where people go who are really,
"Down in the Dumps?"

KEEP YOUR EYE ON THE BALL

A Mom was playing catch with her son and said to him,

"Remember to keep your **"Eye on the Ball."**

When she threw the ball back to him, he immediately put the ball over his eye.

Trying not to laugh, she realized that he did exactly what she asked him to do.

SANTA CLAWS

A Mom shared her sadness after learning why her son
was so scared of having his picture
taken at the Mall with
"Santa Claws".

125

YOUR STORIES

Write your experiences of Unintentional Humor:

_____
_____
_____
_____
_____
_____
_____
_____
_____
_____
_____
_____
_____
_____
_____
_____
_____
_____
_____
_____
_____
_____

YOU CAN SHARE YOUR
STORIES ON OUR WEBSITE:
www.CelebrateAutism.com

GLOSSARY

GLOSSARY

DEFINITIONS

FUNNY BONE: This is not actually a bone, but a point on your elbow where the ulnar nerve runs over the humerus bone. (Humerus sounds like humorous = funny) When you hit this spot it gives a very weird, tingling sensation, and it is not funny at all.

PLAYING MUSIC BY EAR: This describes someone that can play music after listening to it, without looking at any notes. Some people also say that you are "Playing it by Ear," if you are doing something that is unplanned.

COUCH POTATO: This describes someone that leads a very inactive lifestyle. This is usually a person who spends a lot of time on the couch watching television.

KEEP YOUR EYE ON THE BALL:
This is a way of telling someone to stay alert and pay close attention to what is happening around them. It may be said when you are playing a sport and need to catch or hit a ball.

CUT A RUG:
This is a slang expression for dancing. It originates from the idea that you may have to move rugs out of the way to dance or can describe someone who dances so much that they wear a hole in the rug.

STOP BUGGING ME:
This is said when someone is bothering you. It comes from the word, "pester." Bugs are also known as pests, which is where this expression gets its meaning.

<u>BULL IN A CHINA CLOSET:</u> This describes a person that is causing trouble or breaking things. China is fragile dishware and a strong bull would cause a lot of damage if allowed near it. It can also mean aggressiveness or pushiness.

<u>YOU ARE IN THE DOG HOUSE:</u> This is said about a person that is in trouble or someone is very angry with. If a dog has misbehaved, they may be forced to stay in their dog house, which is most likely a punishment.

<u>BROKEN RECORDS:</u> A way to recognize higher levels of achievement than have not been met before. It can be used in reference to sports records and weather temperatures, among other things.

145

<u>RAINING CATS & DOGS</u>: A way to describe the weather when it is raining very hard. There is no clear understanding of where this expression originated--because it really doesn't make sense at all.

<u>SURFING THE WEB:</u> Someone that is on the internet-formally known as the World Wide Web (www.), commonly called the Web. Surfing is the verb that describes searching through channels or networks for information, not riding waves.

<u>MONKEY BUSINESS:</u> This describes someone that is being mischievous, annoying and not behaving properly. It can also be said about someone that is clowning around or being disrespectful.

<u>A FROG IN YOUR THROAT</u>: This describes a person with a hoarse or croaky sounding voice. It sometimes happens to people who are are sick or have laryngitis.

<u>ALL EARS</u>: This is said to a person who is expected to listen closely, not to miss a thing. Someone could also say, "All Eyes", which means to look and watch closely.

<u>BROKEN HEART</u>: A way to describe someone that is very sad or lonely. It may be used when a couple breaks up or when a person very close to you dies.

<u>YOU'RE PULLING MY LEG:</u> A way to refer to someone that is teasing you or playing a joke on you. It could also be said about a person that you think is lying to you.

<u>CHILL OUT:</u> People use this expression to tell someone that they should calm down and not be upset. It may be said to a person that is very scared or nervous about something.

<u>HIT THE SACK:</u> This is common saying for someone that is going to bed. It originated long ago when people slept on sacks of hay, before they had mattresses. People sometimes say, "Hit the Hay", which means the same thing.

CAT'S GOT YOUR TONGUE: This describes someone that is having a hard time thinking of what to say, or is not able to answer a question quickly. Some people may think your silence is suspicious.

NO CRYING OVER SPILLED MILK: This means that you should not get upset over things that are not important or have already happened, because usually there is nothing you can do to change them.

THE FUNNY FARM: This is a slang term used for a mental institution or a place where people go when they are having mental problems. Sometimes these people are considered, "funny in the head".

149

<u>IN A NUT SHELL</u>: This is said if you are describing something in a very brief or concise way. If you don't want to hear all of the details of a story you might say, "just tell me in a nutshell."

<u>HAPPY CAMPER:</u> An informal way to describe someone that is very happy or satisfied. It could also be used to describe a person who is unhappy, by saying; "Not a Happy Camper".

<u>T.V. DINNER:</u> Frozen pre-made meals that come in serving trays that can be easily warmed and eaten off of your lap or on a small table. Many people eat these while watching T.V.

<u>HOLD UP A BANK:</u> The definition of a "hold up" is a delay, or informally it means an attempt to rob (or steal) from someone with a weapon. It is common to refer to a bank robbery as a, "Bank Hold Up".

<u>DON'T LET THE BED BUGS BITE:</u> This saying is part of a popular nursery rhyme & poem that has been said to children before going to sleep for years. Although, there are real bed bugs that can live in mattresses, you probably don't have them.

<u>CAR POOLS:</u> In this term the word pool means grouping together resources for a common advantage. People who share rides in the same car save fuel and money and help the environment by emitting less gas pollutants.

151

JELLYFISH: Jellyfish are one of the oldest living creatures, with over 350 known species, occupying every ocean on the planet. It is NOT where jelly is made and they are actually not even a fish.

OPEN A CAN OF WORMS: This is a way of saying that you may create new problems while trying to solve others. It is often used to warn of complicated matters by saying; "Don't Open that Can of Worms."

YOU STOOD ME UP: This describes a person who you have made plans with that doesn't show up, leaving you alone waiting for them, and usually very angry.

TURN INTO A PRUNE: After spending a long time in water, people's fingers and toes swell and become very wrinkly. It looks similar to a prune. A prune is a wrinkly fruit- actually a dried plum.

PIECE OF CAKE: This is a common way to refer to something that is considered very easy. The saying originated during World War II by British soldiers who said the expression, "Easy as Pie," which means the same thing.

TIME FLIES WHEN YOU'RE HAVING FUN: This expression is often said if you feel that time is passing quickly, because you are enjoying yourself.

153

THE WRONG SIDE OF THE BED:
This may be said about someone that is having a very bad day. Most commonly said in the morning, especially if a person wakes up in a bad mood.

WILD GOOSE CHASE:
This saying is used if you feel you have wasted time searching for something that cannot be found. It was used by Shakespeare to describe following someone on an erratic course.

HORSEPLAY:
This describes rough play, fooling around, fake wrestling or many different types of "kids play". Based on the knowledge that young horses like to frolic, run and charge to release energy. It also may be called, "Horsing Around".

LET THE CAT OUT OF THE BAG:
The expression was used to describe a dishonest merchant promising a pig but selling a cat. Most people use it to refer to someone who reveals a secret without meaning to.

FOREFATHERS:
The confusion with this is the word 'FORE', which sounds like the number four (4). A Forefather is a member of a past generation who contributed to a common cause. Much of our history came from our Forefathers.

FINGER FOODS:
Food that is eaten directly from your hands, rather than food eaten with a fork & knife or other utensils. Examples of finger foods are; pizza, fried chicken, french fries, and hamburgers.

<u>ELBOW GREASE:</u> This describes working very hard, especially at manual labor. It is not an oil or cream that can be used to achieve positive results, but rather the hard work and effort you must put in for great accomplishments.

<u>BACKSEAT DRIVER:</u> Someone who is a passenger in a car that insists on telling the driver how to operate the vehicle, even though they are not the one who is driving.

<u>DUCK TAPE:</u> Also known as "Duct Tape", it is very strong, flexible tape with a cloth backing. It is usually gray or black in color and is commonly used by the military. It is water resistant and has many uses.

POTLUCK DINNER: A gathering of people where each person or group of people contributes a dish of food to be shared among the group. This is common way for people to have a party.

GOLF NUT: People are often referred to as a, "nut", when they are extremely devoted to a particular interest. It can be used in many different ways; motorcycle nut, history nut, sports nut.

CLOUD NINE: This is a common way of describing great happiness. It comes from the weather bureau's rating of clouds. A large cloud is rated a nine (9) when it reaches over 40,000 feet.

PIG OUT: This describes someone that has eaten way too much food. Sometimes people like the food so much that they eat more than they should and actually make themselves sick.

LAME DUCK: This refers to an elected official who is still in office but has not been re-elected. In the U.S.A., the President can only serve two terms, and is often called a Lame Duck in the 2nd term.

DOG EARED PAGES OF A BOOK: The folded down corners of book pages, which is often done to mark your place. It also can be said when describing a worn out or overused book.

THAT GIRL IS HOT: This is a slang term about someone who is very attractive and enjoyable to look at. It can be said about both men and women. It is not the same as hot which describes the temperature.

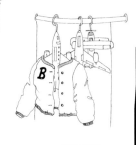

AIRPLANE HANGARS: A hangar is a closed structure that protects airplanes and spacecraft. It is spelled differently from hangers which is what you use to hang your clothing on.

CATCHING RAYS: A narrow beam of light is known as a ray, and sunlight is often called rays. People who are suntanning or spending time in the sun often say that they are "Catching Rays".

CAT FISH: This is a group of ray-finned fish that come in many shapes and sizes. They all have distinctive barbels by their mouth, which look like the whiskers on a cat.

RECYCLE YOUR TREE: In recent years, it has become common for people to recycle their Christmas trees. The trees are put through a machine that grinds them and turns them into garden mulch, but they are not used as trees again.

HIT THE BIRDIE: In the game of Badminton, the shuttlecock is often referred to as the, "Birdie" because it is made out of real feathers. In competition, it has 16 feathers, which usually come from the left wing of a goose.

COMPUTER MOUSE: A hand held device that controls the cursor on a computer screen. It is called a mouse because some people think it looks like one with a small body and the cord as the tail.

DOWN IN THE DUMPS: This saying has been used for hundreds of years to describe feelings of sadness or depression. The dump is also a place where large amounts of trash are taken, but they are not the same.

YOU'RE A CHICKEN: This is a common way to describe someone that is afraid or scared. Chickens are considered cowardly animals because they usually run away when people approach them.

161

CARD SHARK: Someone who is very skilled at playing cards is often called a "Card Shark". Since they often win, people may think they are cheating. A person good at billiards may be called a, "Pool Shark".

YOU'RE DRIVING ME UP THE WALL: This is said when someone is really bothering or annoying you and you want to climb the walls to escape them. A person may also say, "You're driving me Crazy," which means something very similar.

THE MONKEY BARS: Playground equipment is sometimes referred to as "Monkey Bars", because of the many ways children can climb and swing on them, similar to what monkeys do in the wild. This may also be called a "Jungle Gym".

<u>UNDER THE WEATHER</u>: This describes a person who is sick or not feeling well. Because some people believe that bad weather can make you sick, people use this term to describe someone who is ill.

<u>SCHOOL OF FISH</u>: A group of fish are called a "school". Fish swim together in schools as protection from predators, and to more easily find food. (They also are smarter when they are in school!!)

<u>FISHING TACKLE</u>: All of the gear that is used for fishing is called the tackle. Items such as hooks, lures, weights and line are often kept in a container called a "Tackle Box".

163

CONTACT US

<u>CONTACT INFORMATION</u>

Thank you for helping us
Celebrate the Literal Mind of Autism.

We are currently at work
on our next book.
If you are interested in
sharing your stories and
having them included in
Unintentional Humor Vol. 2,
contact us by email:

CelebrateAutism@gmail.com

or through our website:

www.CelebrateAutism.com

Please connect with us:

As Autism diagnoses continue to rise at astronomical rates, more funds are needed to support research and improved treatments.
The net proceeds from book sales will be donated to Autism groups around the country.

If you would like to use this book to raise funds for your Autism Organization, Please contact Linda Anderson;
lindagundanderson@gmail.com
or download an application on our website:
www.CelebrateAutism.com

Thank you for sharing this book with others.
Together we will increase Autism awareness.
Awareness Brings Change!